DISCARDED

LET'S VISIT WALES

Let's visit
WALES

GEORGE H. HAINES

BURKE

First published November 1975
Second revised edition 1984
© George H. Haines 1975 and 1984

ACKNOWLEDGEMENTS

The author and publishers are grateful to the following for permission to reproduce copyright
illustrations:
  Peter Baker; British Steel Corporation; British Transport Docks Board; Central
  Electricity Generating Board; City of Cardiff; C. M. Dixon; National Coal Board;
  The Wales Tourist Board; The Welsh Office.
They are also grateful to other authorities who assisted in supplying information.

CIP data
Haines, George H.
  Let's visit Wales. – 2nd ed.
/ 1. Wales – Social life and customs – Juvenile literature
  I. Title
  942.9085'7   DA711.5
  ISBN 0 222 01029 0

Burke Publishing Company Limited
Pegasus House, 116–120 Golden Lane, London EC1Y 0TL, England.
Burke Publishing (Canada) Limited
Registered Office: 20 Queen Street West, Suite 3000, Box 30, Toronto, Canada M5H 1V5.
Burke Publishing Company Inc.
Registered Office: 333 State Street, PO Box 1740 Bridgeport, Connecticut 06601, U.S.A.
Filmset in "Monophoto" Baskerville by Green Gates Studios Ltd., Hull, England.
Printed in Singapore by Tien Wah Press (Pte.) Ltd.

Contents

WALES

CYMRU

ST. DAVID'S H

NATIONAL PARKS

LAND OVER 300 metres
approx. 1,000 feet

Carew Cross in South Wales—a reminder of the old Celtic
Christianity

Wales and the Welsh People

On the map Wales is shown as a small piece of land jutting out from the west side of England. It is so small that many people speak of "England and Wales" in one breath as if they were one country. The two countries share the same Government. They have the same laws. They use the same currency. For many purposes they are one. But the visitor driving along one of the roads from England into Wales quickly discovers that Wales considers itself to be a separate country. By the roadside at the border he will see a sign saying *Croeso i Gymru*—"Welcome to Wales". The Post Office vans have "Royal Mail" on one side and *Post Brenhinol* on the other. You are made aware that you are in another country.

The area of Wales is 20,764 square kilometres (8,017 square miles), compared with the area of England which is 130,362 square kilometres (50,333 square miles). The population of Wales is 2.8 million. Greater London alone has two and a half times more people than the whole of Wales.

How is it that such a small country should be so independent? To find the answer we must look back into history.

The story of early Britain is one of waves of invaders. In the sixth and seventh centuries before Christ the Celts came to Britain and spread to all parts including Wales. The Romans invaded Britain in A.D. 43. They swept across the country quickly and reached the Severn Valley near the Welsh border by A.D. 51. It was more than twenty-five years later

The remains of the Roman amphitheatre at Caerleon built in the first century A.D.

before they had conquered Wales. Even then they only held a number of strong points. The Celts retreated to the mountains. They retained their customs and traditions.

After four hundred years the Romans withdrew. Other invaders followed. For several centuries England was divided into separate kingdoms. But the invaders never subdued the Celts in Wales.

At the end of the eighth century Offa became the most important ruler in England. He ruled many of the little kingdoms. Even he could not conquer Wales. So he had a great earth ditch and bank built as a line to mark a border between England and Wales. This is called Offa's Dyke.

The Normans under William the Conqueror invaded England in 1066. They too found the Celts were a problem. The Normans were able to gain some ground in the flatter country of South Wales. They were not able to conquer the more mountainous areas to the north. William the Conqueror gave land along the border to some of his knights and told them to hold this as a barrier against the Welsh. This land became known as the Border Marches.

It was not until 1282 that Edward I made a final effort to conquer Wales. He built a line of great castles to subdue the country. From that time Wales ceased to have any separate political existence. But there were constant rebellions.

Peace between the two nations came in a strange way as the result of a romance between Catherine, widow of Henry V of England, and Owen Tudor, a squire from Anglesey. Owen Tudor had fought at Agincourt and been given a position at court. When the king died, Owen Tudor and Catherine married. They had three sons. Many years passed and then in 1485 a grandson of this couple came to the throne of England. He was Henry VII—a king born in Wales with Welsh blood. It might almost be said that Wales had conquered England! The Tudor kings righted many of the wrongs about which the Welsh had complained.

So we see that the Welsh people are the descendants of the Celts who were among the earliest people in Britain. Over the centuries they have resisted many invaders. Even today many people in Central and North Wales speak Welsh, which

11

is a Celtic language. There are Welsh radio and television programmes. In the streets you hear the greeting *Bore da*— "Good day". When you hear the Welsh sing *Sospan Fach* or some other Welsh song at a rugby match you know that Wales is still a separate country at heart.

Although Wales is a small country it is full of variety. Along the south coast is a rich plain where the winters are very mild. In the interior, the land is mountainous with some peaks more than 915 metres (3,000 feet) high which are often snow-covered. At the holiday resort of Llandudno on the North Wales coast the average rainfall is 762 millimetres (30 inches) a year. In the mountains less than thirty-two kilometres (twenty miles) inland there is usually about 380 centimetres (150 inches) of rain in a year.

Most of Wales is sparsely populated. Two thirds of the people live in the south-eastern counties of West, Mid and South Glamorgan and Gwent. In these counties are the three biggest towns—Cardiff (280,000 inhabitants), Swansea (188,000) and Newport (134,000).

In most of Wales agriculture is the main industry. However there are two important industrial areas—in the north-east and in the south-east. The output of these areas is so great that it makes Wales one of Britain's most important industrial regions. The whole of Britain's anthracite and much of its steam coal and other specialised coals are mined in the south-east. The iron- and steel-works produce thirty per cent of Britain's output. Almost all of Britain's output of tinplate and

The modern colliery at Abernant, South Wales

much of its sheet steel is made in Wales. The aluminium industry of Wales produces over half of Britain's aluminium sheet. One quarter of Britain's oil refining capacity is at Milford Haven on the South Wales coast.

This great industrial activity is concentrated into such a small part of the country that for many people Wales is a place for holidays. It has over 1,200 kilometres (750 miles) of coastline. It has mountains to climb and moorlands to explore. Of the ten National Parks created in Britain to protect areas of great beauty, three are in Wales.

The Welsh are proud of their country, and they have a country to be proud of.

The Welsh Language

Before going further we had better look at the Welsh language. Most of the place names in Wales are in Welsh. Some of these appear to be unpronounceable to those who cannot speak Welsh. It will be easier to read these names if some simple rules are noted.

Welsh is a phonetic language and it is regular. Once the rules are learnt there are only rare exceptions.

A sign in Welsh and English. It points along Offa's Dyke Long Distance Path which follows the line of the old Dyke

Consonants

b, d, h, l, m, n, p and *t* are pronounced in the same way as in English.

c is always hard as *k*

ch is pronounced as in the Scottish word "lo*ch*"

dd is *th* as in "*th*is"

f is pronounced as *v*

ff is pronounced as *f*

g is hard as in *g*oal

ll is the most difficult sound. The nearest English-speaking people can get is *thl*

r is trilled as the Scots pronounce it

s is hard as in *s*ong

j, k, q, v, x and *z* are not found in Welsh.

Vowels

	short	*long*	*never*
a	as in th*a*t	as in *a*h	as in m*a*de
e	as in g*e*t	as in l*a*te	as in m*ee*t
i	as in p*i*n	as in w*ee*d	as in l*i*ne
o	as in g*o*t	as in sc*o*re	as in t*o*n
u	as in w*i*g		as in th*u*d
w	as in s*oo*t	as in sch*oo*l	

y has two sounds. In the final syllable of words, and usually when it is in words of one syllable, it is sounded as the *i* in d*i*d; in other cases it is sounded as the *u* in g*u*n.

15

As Welsh is a phonetic language every letter should be sounded. There are no silent letters as there are in some English words.

The accent is usually on the second last syllable—Deganwy = Degan*oo*i

Place names are usually descriptive. Some parts of names are seen frequently and will be recognised:

Aber—means mouth or estuary: Aberdovey—the mouth of the River Dovey

Betws—chapel: Betws-y-coed—the chapel in the wood

Llan—church enclosure: Llanrwst—the place round the church of St Gwrst

Dol—meadow: Dolgarrog—the meadow of the torrent

The longer names which look very difficult to pronounce can be learnt by first going over them syllable by syllable and then taking a deep breath and putting the whole name together.

The Land of Wales

Wales is the largest western-facing peninsula of Britain. It juts out to the west between the mouth of the River Severn in the south and the mouth of the River Dee in the north. The south of Wales is on about the same latitude as London. The extreme north of the country is just south of the latitude of Liverpool.

Wales is bounded by the sea on the north, west and south. The west side curves in a great crescent shape known as Cardigan Bay. Off the north-west corner of Wales is the island of Anglesey. On the map it looks like a football bouncing off the head of a player.

On the east the border with England runs beside the counties of Cheshire, Shropshire, Hereford and Worcester, and Gloucestershire. For many centuries there was confusion as to whether Gwent (formerly Monmouthshire) was in Wales or England. For some purposes it was regarded as an English county; for others it was regarded as part of Wales. To make sure that there was no doubt it was necessary to refer to "Wales and Monmouthshire" in legal documents and when giving figures of areas or population. Under the re-organisation of the counties made by the Local Government Act 1972, Monmouthshire has been included as part of Wales. It is now called Gwent.

If you look at a coloured contour map of Wales you will see than many areas are coloured brown to indicate that they

Snowdonia: the area is often green and beautiful . . . . . .

are high. About a quarter of the country is over 305 metres (1,000 feet) high. The only low-lying land is in the narrow coastal belt and the valleys of the rivers.

The highest land is in the north-west in Snowdonia. This is the area around Snowdon, 1,085 metres (3,560 feet) high, the highest mountain in England and Wales. The mountains run south through the centre of Wales. This mountainous country is what many people picture when they think of Wales. It is a beautiful area. Proud peaks reach up to the sky. After rain their sides are streaked with the silvery strands of streams rushing down to fill lakes or join rivers.

By world standards they are not very great mountains. Eight Snowdons piled on top of each other would not be as high as Mount Everest. Compared with the hills of England the area seems very wild. Travellers have been impressed by its beauty for centuries. But you cannot eat beauty. The mountain sides are too rocky and steep to be used for farming other than rearing sheep. This part of the country has always had few people.

. . . . . . **although the mountain summits are rocky and snow-covered**

The narrow strip along the coast of North Wales has much less rain than the mountains. It has many sunny days. This coast has developed into a holiday area. Much of it is within easy reach of the big English cities of Manchester and Liverpool. The people of those cities regard the North Wales coast as a playground for weekends or longer holidays.

The island of Anglesey is separated by the narrow Menai Straits from North-west Wales. The road goes over the Menai Bridge built in 1826 by Thomas Telford. The railway goes over the Britannia Bridge. This was built in 1850 by Robert Stephenson. In 1970 it was severely damaged by fire. It has since been rebuilt and a road deck has been added above the railway. The railway continues to Holyhead which is on its own little island off the western extremity of Anglesey. From the harbour, boats go to Ireland.

South Stack lighthouse, Holyhead, Anglesey

The coast of Anglesey, often exposed to stormy seas

Anglesey is 715 square kilometres (276 square miles) in area. The island is flat compared with the Welsh mainland. There is little land over 180 metres (600 feet) high. The island has a coastline of nearly 190 kilometres (118 miles). This has many little bays; some are sandy, others have huge rocky headlands. Anglesey has a mild climate. It is rarely very cold in winter, and it avoids the hottest weather of summer. In the interior there are many farmers keeping herds of dairy or beef cows.

The island is exposed to the full fury of the Atlantic winds. Many of the older whitewashed cottages are very low. They seem to be crouching to avoid the wind. Ships at sea here are often in danger. There have been many wrecks. In 1859 the *Royal Charter* bringing passengers from Australia was wrecked off Anglesey and 465 people were drowned.

21

The peak of land jutting out at the north-west corner of Wales is called the Lleyn Peninsula. Farms and villages here are small. There are quiet little bays along the coast.

The strip of land between the mountains and the sea along the coast of Cardigan Bay is narrow in the north. The rivers there have long narrow estuaries lined with wooded hills. Aberystwyth at the centre of the bay is called the "capital of Mid Wales". It has many administrative offices and a University college. This gives it a rather serious air, but the crowds of holiday-makers on the beach dispel this feeling.

The coastal strip becomes less hilly and wider in the south. At the southern end of Cardigan Bay a large peninsula juts out into the Atlantic. At the peak is St David's Head. There are exciting cliffs round the coast.

The climate in South-west Wales is very mild and the Spring flowers come earlier than in most parts of Britain. There are many mixed farms where crops are grown and dairy cows kept. In the nineteenth century milk from farms in this area was on sale in London every morning, thanks to a good rail service. Now large factories take the milk from the farms to make butter and cheese.

Milford Haven is a great natural harbour. Pembroke Dock used to be one of the chief Royal Naval Dockyards. In the eighteenth century wooden warships were built there. Now the harbour is important as an oil terminal.

The South-east of Wales differs from any of the regions we have looked at so far. This is the area where two-thirds of the people of modern Wales live. It has the largest cities—Cardiff, Swansea and Newport. It is an industrial area. The rest of Wales is rural countryside.

This difference is due to the fact that coal was found in the valleys where the streams come down from the mountains to the sea. In the sixteenth and seventeenth centuries the coal was exported. When the industrial revolution came in England the ready supply of coal fuel encouraged the production of iron and steel in this part of Wales. In a few years villages became busy towns. Now the steel-works of South Wales produce thirty per cent of Britain's output. Other industries have grown up in this area and it has become one of the most important industrial regions of Britain.

The eastern side of Wales along the border with England includes several different types of country. In the north, round Flint and Wrexham, is the second industrial area of Wales. Like that in South Wales it is based on a coal-field. There was an early iron industry in this area but it did not have the advantage of easy transport by sea. Canals and later the railways were built as a means of transport. As in South Wales, other industries have been encouraged to move to the area. These include manmade fibre works at Holywell.

The central area of the borderland is remote countryside. It has not the dramatic mountains of the land to the west, nor the industrial activity of the two areas we have just looked at. Much of the land is around 305 metres (1,000 feet) high and there are vast stretches of moorland. This is largely sheep-rearing country with farms forming into little villages. Small towns are busy on market days.

With the adjoining parts of Shropshire, and Hereford and Worcester this forms one of the few areas of Britain where life still goes on at an easy pace. Some of the best stretches of Offa's Dyke are to be seen very near to the present-day border. A ditch and a bank built a thousand years ago to mark the boundary between Wales and England, it remains in this unchanging countryside as a symbol from the past.

In the south the borderland rises to the exciting mountains of the Brecon Beacons, a National Park area. This is not so dramatic as the mountainous region of Snowdonia. It has the peace and quiet of the border area. Fewer people visit it. Here you can see Wales as it was before it became popular with holiday-makers.

Gradually the borderland merges into the industrial area

The Brecon Beacons area—the mountains are less rugged than in Snowdonia

of the south-east. In the late eighteenth century coal-mining and iron-working industries began here.

Most of the rivers of Wales are short. They rush headlong from the mountains to the sea. After heavy rain they increase rapidly in size. Then as quickly they dwindle again.

The two largest rivers to rise in Wales start on Plynlimmon in Central Wales. Plynlimmon is 752 metres (2,468 feet) high and only nineteen kilometres (twelve miles) from the coast of Cardigan Bay. The rivers flow eastwards *away* from the sea.

The Severn which is the longest river in Britain flows north-eastwards to Shrewsbury in Shropshire. After looping round this town it turns and flows southwards until it reaches the sea near Bristol. Its total length is 354 kilometres (220 miles).

The other long river which rises on Plynlimmon is the Wye. This flows eastwards into Hereford and Worcester and goes to the city of Hereford. Then it turns southwards to join the Severn near Chepstow. The Wye is 217 kilometres (135 miles) long. The lower portion of its valley from Monmouth to its junction with the Severn is one of the most famous beauty spots of Britain.

The third longest river to rise in Wales is the Dee. This starts in Lake Bala, the largest natural lake in Wales. The Dee also flows eastwards. It goes through Llangollen into Cheshire. There it turns northwards and loops out towards the sea.

Although Wales is a small country it has many different types of countryside and many surprises.

The Castles of Wales

During the long period of fighting between the English and the Welsh many castles were built. Some of these can still be seen.

The most impressive are a chain in North Wales built by King Edward I of England after his conquest of Wales in 1282. Along the border with England are the castles of the lords of the Border Marches. Some of these are in England. There are other Norman castles in South Wales. In the mountain areas there are the remains of the castles of the Welsh princes. Most of these are not as imposing as the castles built by the English because the Welsh princes were not very rich.

The castles built by Edward I are at Flint, Rhuddlan, Conwy, Beaumaris, Caernarfon, Harlech and Aberystwyth. You will see from the map that these are all on the coast or by large rivers. This was so that supplies could be taken to them by ship if the castles were under attack from the Welsh.

A view of Rhuddlan Castle built by King Edward I, strategically positioned on the river bank

**Conwy Bridge
and Castle**

The castles of Flint and Rhuddlan were built first. They are now in a very ruined condition. Conwy Castle is an impressive sight. It stands at the mouth of the River Conwy. It has eight grand towers and looks very strong. From the castle a wall 1,280 metres (1,400 yards) long encircles the old town. This is the most complete town wall still standing in Britain. From the top of the castle the line of the wall can be seen. Some people say that it is in the shape of a harp. Every road leaving the town has to pass through the wall. Some roads go through the old gateways. For other roads arches have been built in modern times. In front of the castle is the suspension bridge built in 1826 by Thomas Telford. This matches the castle so well that it appears to be part of it.

Beaumaris Castle is on the eastern coast of the island of Anglesey. When Edward selected the site he ordered the Welsh people who were living near by to move away. They went to Newborough on the other side of the island. He then built the castle and made a new English settlement. Beaumaris is the best of the castles built by Edward I. There is an outer defensive wall. Inside this is the castle itself with a higher wall. This enabled defenders to fire over the heads of those on the outer wall. The moat of the castle is connected to the sea. Ships with supplies were able to sail right up to the walls of the castle.

The castles of Harlech and Caernarfon are in the west of Wales.

Harlech Castle

Caernarfon Castle

Harlech Castle was built on a rocky crag. It now overlooks low ground on which there is a golf course. When the castle was built the sea covered this land. It still makes a grand sight although it now has no roof and is partly in ruins.

Harlech Castle was involved in many battles. The rousing song *Men of Harlech* which is sung in many British schools is said to have been inspired by a siege in 1468. Even after the settlement with the Welsh the castle saw action. It was the last Lancastrian fortress to fall in the Wars of the Roses. In the seventeenth-century Civil War between Parliament and the King it was also the last fort to surrender.

In 1969 Caernarfon Castle was seen on television by many people when it was the scene of the investiture of H.R.H. Prince Charles as Prince of Wales. The castle stands at the estuary of the River Seiont. It has the river on one side and the Menai Straits on the other. It has a more gracious appearance than the other castles built by King Edward I. It has nine towers which are surmounted by turrets. The grandest of these is the Eagle Tower which has three turrets. Caernarfon is larger than the other castles built by Edward I and it had

29

more living accommodation. It was intended to be the palace of the King's representative in Wales and the administrative headquarters of the territory.

In 1284 Edward II was born in the castle. In that year the Welsh nobles told Edward I that they would never yield obedience "to any other than a prince of their own nation, of their own language and whose life and conversation was spotless". It is said that Edward replied that he would appoint a prince "who was born in Wales, who could speak not a word of English and whose life and conversation nobody could stain". He then presented them with his infant son. He certainly fulfilled the conditions made by the Welsh, although not in the way they had intended! By tradition this took place at Caernarfon Castle. It is now believed that if it did occur at all, the event took place at Rhuddlan castle. As at Conwy, there are the remains of the town wall, but they are not so impressive.

These castles built by Edward I are the most perfect examples of medieval fortification in Britain. They show the peak of the art of castle-building. By comparison, the castles of the rest of Wales do not appear so impressive.

Pembroke Castle in South Wales has a fine position on a rocky peninsula on the coast. It is on a site which had been occupied for defensive purposes before the castle was built. The most striking feature is a circular keep 9.14 metres (thirty feet) in diameter with walls 2.74 metres (nine feet) thick. This was so strong that attempts to blow it up during the Civil War failed.

Pembroke Castle earned a strange fame in the Civil War. After Parliament had secured victory Oliver Cromwell ordered his forces to be disbanded. John Poyer, the mayor of Pembroke, who had fought for the Parliamentarians was disgruntled with the terms. He declared that he would hold the castle. As a result, Cromwell himself came down to command the forces in this second "mini Civil War" against a castle which had fought for him for five years. John Poyer was later shot—a tragic fate for a loyal supporter.

Another striking castle in South Wales is Caerphilly. This is eleven kilometres (seven miles) north of Cardiff. It has a long history. The Romans had built a fort near by. Later the site was fortified by the Welsh. When the Normans came they quickly conquered the low land to the south of Caerphilly.

Caerphilly Castle

The area round the castle remained in Welsh hands until 1266. Then Earl Gilbert de Clare ejected the Welsh and took over the castle.

It was Earl Gilbert who built the present castle. He also constructed lakes as defences. The castle covers in all an area of 9.31 hectares (twenty-three acres). In Britain only Windsor Castle is larger in size.

When the Normans came to Gwent, they built a number of castles to hold back the Welsh. There was one at Monmouth and others at Grosmont, Skenfrith and Raglan. Ruins of all these can still be seen. Raglan became the greatest.

The building of the present castle was commenced in about 1430 by Sir William ap Thomas (*ap* appears in many early Welsh names and means "son of"). The work was continued by his son William Herbert. William Herbert gained great wealth. For his part in supporting the Yorkist side in the Wars of the Roses he gained favour with the King and was granted the title of Earl of Pembroke. To match his power he extended the castle and added to its glory. By the end of the fifteenth century it was one of the most imposing buildings in the country. During the following centuries the family continued to grow in importance and the Herberts were great figures at the courts of Queen Elizabeth I and King Charles I. Their allegiance to the crown led to their downfall in the Civil War, for the victory of the Parliamentarians resulted in the castle being destroyed. Even now, however, much remains to be seen. It has the appearance of the home of an important nobleman.

Powis Castle near Welshpool, one of the few castles in Wales which are still inhabited

In the northern part of the border area are Chirk and Powis which were castles of Lords of the Marches. Unlike the other castles we have looked at these are still inhabited. They have been lived in by the same families for over five hundred years.

In contrast to these gaunt ancient buildings is Castell Coch eight kilometres (five miles) from Cardiff. This is a delightful sight with round turrets topped by conical roofs. It is so pleasing that pictures of it are often used in advertisements for Welsh holidays. But it is not an ancient castle at all. It was built as a folly by the third Marquess of Bute in about 1870.

Present-day visitors to Wales enjoy looking at the historic castles. We must remember that to the Welsh people of the time they were the fortresses of a hated enemy.

33

The Singing Welsh

The quickest way to find out about the Welsh people is to visit an *eisteddfod*. You will not be able to understand much of what is going on because everything is in Welsh. This will show you how keenly patriotic about their language the Welsh are. You will probably gather that the event is connected with the arts. There are competitions for poetry, writing and singing. You will see that everyone is excited about the event.

Where else in the world would you find this type of competition arousing such enthusiasm? There is not merely one *eisteddfod* but many—the plural, by the way, is *eisteddfodau* not *eisteddfods*. Many counties and towns throughout the country hold their own *eisteddfod*.

The great event of the year is the National Eisteddfod which is held in North Wales one year and in South Wales the next. This lasts for a whole week and there are many types of competitions. The two most important are for the Chair and the Crown. The Chair is awarded for a poem in a strict and complicated Welsh metre. The Crown is awarded for verse of

A musical drama competition at the National Eisteddfod

The traditional tall black hat and red cloak worn here are now only worn on festive occasions

less formal type. Entries are made under pen names. When the pen name of the winner is announced he must stand up and identify himself.

The *eisteddfod* has a long history. The name means "a gathering of poets". Poets have always been highly regarded in Wales. In early times each prince had his poet, and the poet had special privileges. Some of the poems from very early times have been collected together.

The first *eisteddfod* with competitions was held in 1176 at Cardigan Castle when it was newly built. In 1858 a great *eisteddfod* was held in Llangollen in North Wales. This was such a success that it was decided to hold a National Eisteddfod every year. Even during the 1914-18 and 1939-45 world wars National Eisteddfodau were held.

Nowadays the chief officials wear long druid's robes. This has nothing to do with poetry or the Welsh. The connection began in a strange way. In 1792 the Gorsedd (Assembly) of Druids was started by Edward Williams. He adopted the Welsh name of Iolo Morganwg. He hoped that his meetings would become more important than the *eisteddfodau*. In fact the *eisteddfodau* remained the more popular and the poets adopted the druidic robes. It is a piece of make-believe which adds a touch of romance to the occasion.

The *eisteddfodau* are very Welsh events. They are for Welsh people. In 1947 the people of Llangollen in North Wales decided to allow all the world to share the pleasure of such meetings. They organised a festival with choral, solo and instrumental competitions to which people from any country were invited. Since that first start the event has grown. Now every year people come from countries all over the world. Folk-singing and dancing are included. These displays are very colourful with the competitors wearing their national costumes.

The people of Llangollen provide free accommodation in their homes for the competitors. There are impromptu rehearsals in the streets; the little grey stone town becomes alive with colour and music.

National costume from other countries, like this one, bring a touch of colour to the streets of Llangollen during the eisteddfod

The *eisteddfodau* could only continue in a country of people who love poetry and singing. The Welsh men's choirs of the Valleys are very famous. It is their Celtic ancestry which makes the Welsh so different from their English neighbours.

Nowadays the people of Wales wear clothes similar to other western nations. On special occasions—or for the benefit of tourists—Welsh girls sometimes wear their traditional costumes. These have long red cloaks and tall black hats. In 1797, when a French force invaded South Wales, the commander of the local forces ordered a line of women dressed in this costume to march in and out of sight among the hills. The French mistook them for British red-coated soldiers coming to the attack, so they retreated.

Many Welsh writers and poets are little known outside their country because they wrote in Welsh. However, some who chose to write in English have become famous. One of the best known is T. E. Lawrence (1888-1935), often called "Lawrence of Arabia" because of his adventures in that country. He was born in North Wales. His book *The Seven Pillars of Wisdom* became world famous. An earlier explorer, H. M. Stanley (1841-1904), who is remembered for his search for Dr. David Livingstone in Africa, was also born in North Wales.

W. H. Davies (1871-1940), the "tramp poet" who wrote *The Autobiography of a Super Tramp* was born in Newport, Monmouthshire (now Gwent). Dylan Thomas (1914-1953), whose rolling voice is still heard in recordings on the radio, based *Under Milk Wood* on characters he had met at Laugharne in South Wales. The Welsh novelist Richard Llewellyn has written many best-selling books including *How Green Was My Valley*.

Two outstanding painters from Wales have been Richard Wilson (1714-82) and Augustus John (1878-1961). Wilson studied art in London and Italy and was one of the founders of the Royal Academy in 1768. He specialised in landscapes and is regarded as the father of "English" landscape painting. Augustus John painted modern portraits. Wales has also produced an outstanding architect in Sir Clough Williams-Ellis (1883-1978) who planned and produced the village of Portmeirion on Cardigan Bay. This has a striking mixture of styles and seems like a place in a fairy-tale book.

In this century a number of Welsh actors have become stars of the stage and screen. Ivor Novello (1893-1951) wrote and played in many musical comedies including *The Dancing Years;* Emlyn Williams is an actor who also became well known for his readings of Dickens; while Richard Burton is one of the outstanding stars of the cinema. Harry Secombe, the comedian who has also achieved fame as a singer, is loved by many people and, through television, has become known in most homes throughout the United Kingdom. And we must not forget the two recording stars, Shirley Bassey and Tom Jones, who have shown that talent from Wales can ring round the world.

Politics calls for impassioned speeches at times and several Welshmen have become well known in Parliament. One of Britain's most famous politicians, David Lloyd George (1863-1945), was born in North Wales. He was Prime Minister during the First World War. In more recent times Aneurin Bevan (1897-1960) will be remembered as the creator of the National Health Service. Wales has produced some notable talent.

Work in the Factories

If you go on holiday to Wales you will find it hard to believe that there is any industry in the country. You will take away with you memories of the wonderful mountains or of the glorious beaches. One writer said that most of Wales was populated by sheep and tourists. For centuries Wales was an agricultural country and most of it still remains untouched by industry.

Part of the Welsh countryside still populated only by sheep and tourists—a view in Snowdonia

The industrial areas are only a small part of the country but they are very important.

The main industrial area is a strip in the south-east. This 129 kilometres (eighty miles) long by about forty-eight kilometres (thirty miles) wide. Nearly two-thirds of the people of Wales live in this area. It has most of the mines and great steel-works of Wales. At Milford Haven a great natural harbour has been developed as a centre for the oil industry.

In the north-east of Wales there is another important industrial area with steel-works and manmade fibre plants.

Industry in Wales developed on the coal-fields. In the late eighteenth century ironmasters from England began to work the ironstone in South Wales. They were attracted to the area by the fact that there was coal to smelt the iron, and that there was also the limestone and water needed for the process.

The opening of these works changed the face of the country-side. In 1750 there had been only a few hundred people at Merthyr Tydfil. By 1801 it had a population of 17,000 and was larger than Cardiff, Swansea or any other Welsh town.

At that time the iron produced had to be transported on packhorses. The ironmasters needed better means of transport. They built a canal to Cardiff. In 1804 they saw the first experiment when a "high-pressure train engine" built by Richard Trevithick hauled a ten-tonne load of iron at eight kilometres (five miles) an hour from Merthyr to Abercynon. It was thirty-seven years later when a railway from Merthyr

Tydfil to Cardiff was built by Isambard Brunel.

Until that time most of the coal of South Wales had been used in the local iron-works. The making of the railway provided an easy method to get the coal to the coast. From there it could be shipped to other parts of Britain or to the Continent.

Docks were built along the South Wales coast and many more mines were opened. By 1900 the South Wales coal-field was the busiest in the world.

Young men left the mountains and fields of Wales to earn the higher wages paid in the coal-mines and iron-works. The population of the Rhondda Valley had been only a few hundred in 1850. By 1921 it was 167,000.

In the north-east of Wales around Wrexham another coal-field was discovered and here also iron and steel industries developed.

In the 1920s and 1930s, as other forms of power came into use, the demand for coal began to fall. This produced much unemployment among the miners. The government tried to cure this by encouraging other industries to move to the area. Now there are many types of factory. Products of South Wales include washing-machines, corsets, stockings, biscuits, office furniture, toys, switchgear, oil filters and many other items.

Although the area does not now rely so greatly on coal-mining, it is still an important producer of coal for Britain. The coal-mines of South Wales provide all Britain's anthracite. This is a high-quality coal which is smokeless and leaves

Typical landscape in the Rhondda Valley

little ash when it is burnt. Much of Britain's steam coal is also mined in South Wales. In the late nineteenth century much of it was exported and this led to the growth of docks at Cardiff, Swansea and Newport.

Later when the supply of Welsh iron ore began to run out

A view of the harbour at Port Talbot. It was built to take large ships carrying ore

it became necessary to import ore and this provided additional work for the new docks. These have continued to expand and can now handle the largest ships. At Port Talbot a huge new harbour was opened in 1970. This can be used by ships in excess of 100,000 tonnes. In 1982 the *Cetra Centaurus* entered the harbour with a record cargo of over 126,873 tonnes of iron ore from Australia.

The ports along this coast are also developing other trade. The building of the Severn Bridge has made it easier to carry goods from the port to places in England. Ships prefer to unload their cargoes in South Wales rather than make the journey to London along the English Channel which is becoming dangerously crowded and is often foggy. Special equipment has been installed so that bananas and frozen meat

44

can be unloaded. There is also an important traffic in timber.

One of the fuels which has replaced coal is oil. The ports of South Wales have grown to meet the needs of this trade. British Petroleum established a refinery at Llandarcy near Swansea in 1921. This was the first major refinery in the United Kingdom. For many years tankers went into Swansea Docks to unload the crude oil. As the tankers grew in size another port was needed. Now British Petroleum have an Ocean Terminal at Angle Bay, Milford Haven. This can accommodate huge tankers. The crude oil is pumped ashore and then travels along a pipe line nearly one hundred kilo-metres (sixty-two miles) to the refinery at Llandarcy. Over one thousand tonnes per hour can be sent. The oil takes ten hours to make the journey. Crude oil contains many substances. In the refinery it is separated into its basic parts. Petrol, paraffin, lubricating oil, butane gas, wax and other products are sent from the refinery.

The magnificent natural harbour at Milford Haven has been developed into one of the most important oil terminals in Britain. Nearly one-quarter of Britain's oil enters the port and is refined near by. In addition to British Petroleum other firms operating there include Texaco, Gulf and Amoco.

In looking at these modern developments we must not forget the iron and steel industry. South Wales has been interested in iron for centuries. Iron sheets were being rolled in Wales in the 1780s. In 1860 there were 165 furnaces running in Wales. Steel-making has become the most important

Tugs at work with an oil carrier in Milford Haven

industry of Wales. Ingots are rolled into steel sheet for making cars, refrigerators, and for cladding buildings, and other uses.

The works at Port Talbot extend for some 7 kilometres (over 4 miles). It has four blast furnaces; eighty-four coke ovens; steel converters, continuous casting plant and hot and cold strip rolling mills. The plant dwarfs the men beside it. In forty minutes, the basic oxygen convertor can make enough steel for four hundred motorcars! However, like the castles of old, the new plant is not always considered to be so marvellous by the people of the district. Five hundred men in the new plant do a job once done by two thousand men. The 1,500 men who are not required have to find other jobs.

Most of the steel-making plant is in South Wales, but there is another large plant in the North-east Wales industrial area. This produces galvanised strip, and plastic-coated and prepainted strip.

Other metals are also important in Wales. Aluminium was smelted as long ago as 1909 at Dolgarrog. Now work is con-

46

centrated on rolling aluminium sheet and over half of the total production of Britain comes from Wales.

Wales also has its gold-mines. Although these are no longer worked commercially the gold for royal wedding rings comes from Wales.

The North-east Wales industrial area now produces a variety of goods. As early as 1936 rayon staple fibre was made

Port Talbot, the South Wales steel town

there by Courtaulds. Production is now 1,150 tonnes of fibre a week.

One basic industry which few visitors fail to notice is slate-quarrying. There are quarries near Snowdon. Great heaps of debris from the workings indicate how long these have been worked. The mines at Llechwedd near Blaenau Ffestiniog are now open to the public. You can see how deeply the workers have dug into the heart of the hills since 1765 to bring out slate. The slate is split and used to roof houses. There were also slate-quarries at Prescelly in South Wales. Slates from that area were used on the House of Commons roof which was destroyed in the Second World War.

Wales is lucky that so much industrial activity has been confined to such a small area of the country. The result is that most visitors see nothing of the works and factories.

Work on the Land

As we have seen, the factories of Wales are mostly confined to a small area of the country. The rest is used for farming.

With so much land devoted to farming you might expect that this would be a prosperous industry. In fact, including farmers, managers and part-time workers, there were only 56,000 people engaged in agriculture in Wales in 1982.

This is because much of the land of Wales is not very suitable for farming. Look again at the map and you will see that about one quarter of the land is over 305 metres (1,000 feet) high. Much of this is rocky mountainside or moorland. It has only heather and sparse grass. Crops will not grow on it. Even much of the lower land is too steep for tractors to work on. This land can only be used for rough grazing for sheep. They can pick their way up steep mountainsides. They nibble at the shoots of heather and grass.

About two-fifths of the farmland of Wales is rough grazing of this kind. A further two-fifths is grassland used for grazing sheep and cattle. Only one-fifth can be cultivated for crops.

Dipping sheep on a farm in Mid Wales

Shearing time at a farm in Ceredigion

For many centuries this has been the pattern of farming in Wales. Sheep have been reared on the hills, and cattle reared on the better land. When they are fat enough they are sent to markets in England. In the days before there were trains or lorries, the animals were driven along tracks into England. One road led to London and this is still known in parts of the Midlands as the "Welsh Road".

Now most of the animals are sent to markets along the

border. Oswestry, Shrewsbury and Hereford all have big cattle markets.

Half the farms of Wales are so poor that they do not provide enough work for one man. Some of the farmers have to take other jobs to provide sufficient money for their households. Others struggle along on very little money.

These are the typical farms of the mountains. The farmers live in small stone houses with a few buildings round them. They are mainly sheep farmers. The sheep range the mountains. Every farmer has one or more sheep dogs which are trained to obey shouts or whistles. The Welsh sheep dog is a medium-sized black and white dog with a pointed face. Training a dog takes a long time and a great deal of patience. But a well-trained dog is worth many men in the task of collecting the sheep from the mountainsides. It can run up the slopes faster than the sheep. It will obey the distant whistle of the farmer and bring the whole flock down the hillside, or bring down the one sheep which the farmer wishes to look at more closely.

The hill farmers have a hard life. It is always difficult and dangerous to scramble up the steep mountainside. A fall may lead to serious injury. At any time of the year cloud and rain may come down and visibility is then very poor. In winter, snow may lie deep on the ground for weeks. The farmer and his dog have to go out to make sure that the sheep are safe. Sometimes helicopters have to take hay to the animals.

The farmers of the hills usually have a small amount of low

land to which they take the sheep while the lambs are born. Each farmer marks his sheep with a special mark so that he can recognise them on the open moorland.

The native cattle of Wales are the Welsh Black breed. These are small black cows which are reared for beef.

On the lower land in the south-west there are bigger farms. Here there are a number of famous herds of dairy cows. Nearly half the dairy cattle of Wales are in the county of Dyfed in the south-west. There are now large factories making butter and cheese from the milk of this area.

This part of Wales juts out into the Irish Sea. The warm water of the Gulf Stream keeps the climate very mild. Although there is sometimes frost and snow these do not last very long.

Cattle drinking in the River Glaslyn

This allows the farmers to plant potatoes in February. On most farms in Britain potatoes are not planted till early April. The farmers in South-west Wales can harvest their potatoes in early June. New potatoes from this area appear in the greengrocery shops in England immediately after those from the Channel Islands and they fetch high prices. The farmers plant crops of cauliflowers in the fields after they have dug the potatoes.

Wales is a hard-working place and not the country where you would expect to find exotic foods. Welsh lamb is bought by housewives who know that the joints from the small mountain sheep are very sweet and tender. Caerphilly cheese is another speciality of Wales. This is a soft, white cheese, moist and creamy, which gained favour because it was ideal for the early Welsh miners who worked in a dust-laden atmosphere. The cheese was not made in Caerphilly. It got its name because it was made in the farms in the district around that border town and the farmers brought it to sell in the market there.

In South Wales a curiosity is laver bread. This is not bread at all, but a kind of seaweed! It does not look very attractive, but it is regarded as a great treat by the local folk. It is sold in the markets. It is often mixed with oatmeal and fried in butter or other fat. It can be fried with bacon.

Centuries ago Wales had many dense forests. Now, most of the trees have been cut down. Some were used in ship-building. The wood from many of the smaller trees was made into charcoal for the early iron industry. Later, when coal was used in smelting, trees were cut down to provide pit props. There was little thought for the future.

Therefore Britain has to import much of the timber she needs. The First World War (1914-18) revealed how dangerous it was for Britain to have to rely on wood from overseas. As a result, in 1919, the Government set up the Forestry Commission to plant new forests in Britain. The Commission has to use land which is not suitable for farming. It has acquired 158,000 hectares (390,000 acres) of land in Wales. Much of this is now planted.

The soil and climate of Wales are very suitable for growing trees. Visiting foresters from North America and the continent of Europe are surprised at the rapid growth they see. At Betws-y-coed there is a plantation of Sitka spruce which grew twenty-nine metres (ninety-five feet) high in thirty-eight years.

Some people are disappointed when they return to a favourite place in the mountains and find it covered with trees. The foresters reply that visitors only spend a short time in the area and that it is important for a barren place to be earning money every day as the trees grow.

No doubt, in time we shall get used to the new forests. Meanwhile they are a reminder that the Welsh countryside is a busy place in its own way, even if it appears quiet compared with the industrial area.

A forest in Gwynedd

Power and Water

It is sometimes said that water is Wales' most important export. There is certainly enough of it in the mountainous areas. On Snowdon the average annual rainfall is over 430 centimetres (170 inches) per year. At one time most of this water was wasted. It ran into the rivers. The rivers flowed into the sea. Often the rivers were so full in winter that they burst their banks and flooded. Then they caused damage to farms and houses. Great areas of land beside the River Severn in

55

Shropshire, and in Hereford and Worcester were covered with deep water from the river nearly every winter.

Now water has become valuable. Large quantities are used by the people in towns and cities every day for drinking and washing. Some factories also use great quantities of water. Big cities in England are very pleased to have water from Wales. Every day 364 million litres (eighty million gallons) are supplied to cities in the Midlands. Vast quantities are also supplied daily to Liverpool and other Merseyside towns.

The water is collected in reservoirs. Some of these are natural lakes which have been enlarged so that they hold more water. Many reservoirs are man-made. By building a dam across a river valley it can be made into a reservoir holding huge reserves of water.

The Pen-y-Garreg Dam in the Elan Valley, Powys

The Clywedog Dam and the reservoir which it has created

One of the first reservoirs to be built in Wales to supply an English city was Vyrnwy. In 1881-1888 a dam nearly 50 metres (160 feet) high and nearly 365 metres (1,200 feet) long was built across a valley in the mountains. This made a huge reservoir which covered 560 hectares (1,380 acres). A small village was "drowned" when the new lake was made. New homes were built on higher ground for the people living there. When the water is very low the ruins of the old houses can still be seen. The water from this reservoir is sent through pipes to Liverpool. Now the Forestry Commission has planted trees round the reservoir and it is a beauty spot to which many people go every fine weekend in summer.

In the heart of Wales there are four reservoirs built in the valley of the River Elan. From here, water is piped to Birmingham.

Most of the early reservoirs were built in this way with the water carried to the towns along pipes. Building and repairing the pipes was very expensive.

In 1968 a new kind of reservoir was completed on a tributary of the Severn. A dam 72 metres (237 feet) high was built.

This was the highest dam in Britain. It made a huge reservoir which is used for boating and other recreational purposes.

In winter when the snow melts the streams rush down from the mountains and fill the reservoir. This sudden rush of water used to cause flooding along the banks of the River Severn. Now the water is held back in the reservoir and the danger of flooding is reduced.

When water is wanted by the towns it is not sent along pipes. Instead it is released from the reservoir and flows along the river. The towns wanting water take supplies out of the river. This avoids the need to build a costly pipeline which needs repairing from time to time.

This new type of reservoir reduces the danger of flooding and is also cheaper to operate.

The people of Wales are not so happy about great reservoirs like this. When the valleys are flooded the farmers lose the low land where they used to grow crops and to take their sheep at lambing time. Now they only have the mountain tops left. Some have had to stop farming.

The plentiful supplies of water in Wales are also used in making electricity.

On some bicycles electricity for the lamps is produced by a small dynamo worked by the wheels as they revolve. The electricity generating stations which produce electricity to light our homes work in the same way. They consist of a dynamo and some method of turning it rapidly.

There are three types of power station in Wales.

Each type of power station uses vast quantities of water.

1. Fast-flowing water can be used to turn the dynamo. Stations which work on this system are called hydro-electric power stations.
2. In coal- and oil-fired power stations water is boiled to produce steam which is used to turn the dynamo.
3. In nuclear power stations the heat from nuclear reaction is used to boil water to produce steam which is used to turn the dynamo. Large quantities of water are needed for cooling the plant.

Each of these types of generating station needs large amounts of water. The plentiful supplies of water in Wales makes it ideal for electricity production. There are fifteen power stations in Wales. About one-third of the electricity which they produce is sent by overhead wires to England. This is another way in which the water of Wales helps England.

Some of the earliest power stations were hydro-electric. At Dolgarrog in the Conwy Valley in North Wales a hydro-electric power station was built in 1907 to supply the works and the homes of the workers of the Aluminium Corporation. This was a small plant. Its power was supplied by a fast-flowing river.

Modern hydro-electric power stations are many times larger. They need great supplies of water. Instead of relying on rivers they store water in lakes in the mountains. It is carried down to the power station in large pipes. At the power station it is forced out of a nozzle to turn a turbine, which rotates the generator. The present hydro-electric power station at Dolgarrog takes its water from a lake 359 metres (1,178 feet) above the station. It uses 6,491 litres (1,428 gallons) per second.

Hydro-electric power stations have the advantage that they begin making electricity immediately the water jet is turned on. The other types of power station have to heat up before they can begin to operate. Hydro-electric power stations are therefore very useful to meet sudden demands for power. They provide "instant" electricity.

At Ffestiniog, south of Snowdon in North Wales, there is a pumped storage hydro-electric generating station. This has two reservoirs. One is over 305 metres (1,000 feet) above the power station. The other is beside the power station. When electricity is required, water is released to flow from the upper reservoir to operate the turbine. Then, instead of being allowed to flow away, the water is collected in the lower reservoir. At night when the demand for electricity is low, the water is pumped back to the upper reservoir. It is then ready for use again. The station produces three units of electricity for every four units used to pump the water back to the upper reservoir. The advantage is that the station can be used to produce electricity when it is urgently needed and the pumping can be done at night when there is electricity to spare from the normal types of station.

The Ffestiniog power station, seen across the lower reservoir

This system proved so successful that the Central Electricity Generating Board has built a new pumped storage station at Dinorwig, at Llanberis by Snowdon in North Wales. This is the largest plant of its kind in Europe.

Most power stations have boilers heated by coal or oil. These produce steam which turns a turbine which drives the dynamo. These stations require large amounts of water. In a large boiler 455 litres (one hundred gallons) of water is turned into steam every second! Water is also needed for cooling the generators. A big station needs 182 million litres (forty million gallons) an hour. Much of this is used again after being cooled in the huge cooling towers.

Wales also has two of Britain's nuclear power stations. These operate in the same way as the coal and oil stations. Water is boiled to produce steam to turn the turbine. In the nuclear power stations the heat is produced by nuclear reaction.

A nuclear power station requires large amounts of water. Trawsfynydd was chosen as the site for Britain's first inland nuclear power station because there was a lake there. The station has two reactors, each of which heats six boilers. The station draws 159 million litres (thirty-five million gallons) of water an hour from the lake for cooling. This water is returned to the lake. The warm water raises the temperature of the lake and fish breed very well.

Trawsfynydd—Britain's first inland nuclear power station

There is also a nuclear power station at Wylfa on the north coast of the island of Anglesey. This is built on the sea shore and draws 241 million litres (fifty-three million gallons) per hour from the sea for cooling purposes. These new power stations are tremendous buildings. The main reactor is bigger than Canterbury Cathedral.

The rain water which falls on Wales and fills its rivers and lakes provides very useful supplies of power and water for England.

The Towns and Cities of Wales

Two-thirds of the people of Wales live in the busy south-east corner of the country. It is there that the largest towns are to be found. As we have seen when looking at the industries of Wales these towns grew up quickly in the nineteenth century. They had rows of hastily built brick houses in terraces and were certainly not very pleasant to look at. Like most towns in Britain they are now being modernised and some of them are a surprise to visitors who expect to see the Wales of the 1930s. The traditional towns of Wales are to be found in the country areas. The natural barriers of the mountains isolated these

Grand buildings at the centre of Cardiff, the capital city of Wales

communities and they have a tight compact appearance. The Welsh people are not given to wasting too much time on outward display. This is part of their rather strict religious tradition. Their homes also often look drab outside, but inside there is a sparkling cleanliness. The towns are generally dull-looking places because many of the buildings are built of the local stone and that is dark grey in colour. When you get to know them they are friendly places and the grey stone buildings fit the mountain scene.

Cardiff is the largest city in Wales. Like many of the other towns of the south-east it has grown considerably since the nineteenth century. In 1801 the population was only 1,018; by 1841 it had risen to 10,077; then it grew quickly to 32,954 by 1861; and by 1911 it was 182,280! Today the population is 280,000.

Cardiff is the capital of Wales. Unlike London, the capital of England, it does not have a long history of importance. There was a Roman fort here, but after the Romans left, the site stood desolate until Norman times. The Norman conquerors built a castle. Round this a small town grew up, but it never became very important. In Elizabethan days Cardiff was a haunt for pirates. On one occasion a Sheriff of the town was fined for piracy!

The population figures show that it remained a small place until the middle of the nineteenth century. Then it grew quickly. As its size increased it was granted honours. It was

made a County Borough in 1888. In 1905 it was made a city.
In 1955 it was acknowledged as the capital of Wales.

Because it has grown so quickly, Cardiff is not a place in
which to look for historic buildings. The castle still stands, but
this was altered over the years to become a residence for the
Marquesses of Bute.

The visitor to the city will be impressed by the Civic
Centre. Unlike the civic centres of some British towns this is
not old. The City Hall and Law Courts were built in 1904.
The National Museum of Wales was opened in 1927. Another
fine building is the original portion of the Welsh Office, built

in 1938 to house the former Welsh Board of Health. The large modern extension was built in 1980.

Around these buildings there are pleasant open spaces and there is a park by the riverside. This is one of the most delightful features of the city. Many towns which grew quickly in the nineteenth century did not consider the need for open spaces. Cardiff has preserved a very fine stretch of parks through its centre and this gives it a very pleasant atmosphere.

When you visit the centre of Cardiff you find it so attractive that it is difficult to appreciate that you are in a busy industrial city and port.

The docks at Cardiff grew with the coal trade. But in 1964 the British Transport Docks Board transferred coal shipments to Barry. Now the port area has been modernised to handle other cargoes. Cardiff has become one of the principal fruit ports of the country and it has an important trade in iron ore

The Cardiff Tattoo, with the floodlit castle in the background

International Rugby

and oil as well. There are also paper mills which produce special types of paper.

As the capital city Cardiff is the home of international sport in Wales. The Welsh people are particularly enthusiastic about Rugby and many historic matches have been played at the ground at the National Stadium. Visiting international teams have to face not only the Welsh players but also the intense fervour of the supporters. In 1958 the British Commonwealth and Empire Games were held in Cardiff and for this event the Wales Empire Swimming Pool was built and this provides full international facilities.

Wales' second city is Swansea, which has a population of 188,000. Like Cardiff, Swansea grew quickly with the iron and steel trades in the nineteenth century. It has the advantage of a beautiful site on Swansea Bay. Indeed, in 1804, Swansea was described as a "gay resort of fashion".

To the west of the city the coast curves round to the Mumbles and the Gower Peninsula which is designated as an "Area

68

of outstanding natural beauty" to ensure its protection. The peninsula is thirty-two kilometres (twenty miles) long and varies from five to 6.5 kilometres (three to four miles) wide. Around its coastline there are many beautiful bays to explore, and the interior is delightful for walking.

The centre of Swansea was wiped out in a bombing raid in 1941 and has now been rebuilt. The new civic buildings are striking. They include a Concert Hall decorated with a series of huge wall panels painted by the Welsh artist Frank Brangwyn R.A. (1867-1956). These were designed for the Royal Gallery of the House of Lords, but were acquired by Swansea and are now admired by many people. They illustrate in a very colourful way aspects of the vast British Empire, as it then was, stretching from Canada across Africa and India to Australia.

To the east of the city is the great steel-works of Port Talbot, oil refineries and other factories. This makes a great contrast to the delights of the Gower Peninsula.

Milford Haven in the far south-west of Wales stands on a great natural harbour. The building of the town was commenced in 1793 by Charles Greville, who had received a contract for a naval dockyard there. However, in 1814 the Royal Dockyard was moved to Pembroke Dock on the other side of the inlet which could be better defended. Milford Haven then developed a fishing trade and it became one of the most important fish ports. This trade has now declined.

69

A view of Milford Haven—oil storage and fishing side by side

The great value of the huge natural harbour could not be overlooked. In 1957 the Government announced a scheme to develop Milford Haven as an oil port. Since then development has gone ahead. There are extensive refineries at Milford Haven and now some of the world's largest oil tankers come to the port.

Newport is a busy town at the mouth of the River Usk where it joins the Severn. There has been a town on this site from the earliest days. When the Normans conquered Britain they built a castle, the remains of which can still be seen. There was

70

fighting here several times during the wars between the Welsh and the English. At the beginning of the nineteenth century Newport was still small, but it grew rapidly. You have to look hard to see any signs of Newport's history for it is now a busy modern town. One of the few reminders of the past are some bullet scars on the entrance pillars of the Westgate Hotel which were made during fighting in 1839 when rioters from the Welsh valleys marched into the town. The three ringleaders were transported to Tasmania.

Newport has a busy ironworks at Llanwern. The town owes much of its prosperity to the docks on the River Usk. In addition to cargoes of iron ore and iron products there is a big trade in timber, and the docks have special facilities for the import and export of cars. The river has the highest tidal rise and fall of any river in Britain.

Newport's most famous feature is the striking Transporter Bridge across the river. This was opened in 1906. It has two tall towers linked by a span of over 196 metres (645 feet). A travelling frame runs along the lower side of the span. Cables from the frame support a platform on which cars and passengers are transported from one side of the river to the other. There is no charge to ride across on the platform. If you wish to walk across the upper span you have to pay!

The story of Merthyr Tydfil, which is thirty-nine kilometres (twenty-four miles) north-west of Cardiff, goes back a long way. Like most places in South Wales it has seen great changes. There are traces of a Roman fort below the ground in the park. It appears that the site was deserted after they left. When the Normans came to Britain in 1066 they gradually occupied South Wales, but the district around Merthyr was rarely visited because it was then too wild. Indeed, on one occasion the Welsh from this area raided Cardiff Castle and carried off the governor. He was held captive until he complied with the demands of the Welsh.

The birth of modern Merthyr can be traced to the establishment of the first iron furnace in 1757. The discovery of rich coal and iron deposits in the area led to rapid growth. By the beginning of the nineteenth century it was larger than any other town in Wales.

In the 1920s iron-making was transferred to Cardiff and Port Talbot, and Merthyr's boom began to end. Slowly there has been a change to other industries and now Merthyr makes everything from washing-machines to ladies' tights. In keeping with the new image, the town is being modernised and now has some striking new buildings.

Monmouth, near the border with Hereford and Worcester, is one of the few Welsh towns to retain much of its historic atmosphere. It was the birthplace of King Henry V. There is a statue of him in a niche in the wall of the Shire Hall in Agincourt Square. The old bridge over the River Monnow at the entrance to the town has a fortified gateway. This is the only one still to be seen in Britain.

Monmouth has a strange claim to fame. The people of the town learnt the art of knitting from the Continent of Europe and, in 1540, the first knitted headgear was made in Monmouth. They were known as Monmouth caps. It was thirty years before people in the rest of the country learnt to knit.

Central Wales is mainly a mountainous area and there are few large towns. Most places are small with little stone houses. One of the most delightful is Dolgellau, which lies north of the great mountain Cadair Idris. It is the market town for a wide area. The stone buildings press close on the streets which turn and twist as if trying to dodge the wind. It feels like the most Welsh town in Wales. Here in the heart of the mountain country you meet real Welsh people.

What a contrast to visit Llandrindod Wells. This is almost in the centre of Wales, yet it does not seem Welsh at all. It was mainly built during the last ninety years. It has gracious brick houses standing in wide streets. In the days of Edward VII, eighty thousand visitors a year went to Llandrindod. They stayed in the big hotels and drank the waters from the springs. These have medicinal qualities. Llandrindod was one of several spas in Wales which were famous at the time. The large hotels have now become popular for conferences and this new use brings many visitors.

The main industrial area in North Wales is around Wrexham in the north-east. This is near the English border. At one time there were many collieries, but the number has been reduced over the years. New factories have taken their place and these include an engineering works, a maker of electric cables and a glass fibre producer.

Wrexham has been a market town since the fourteenth century and despite the changes over the years the regular markets are still held. The open air Monday market for general trade is very popular and over 150 stalls are set up.

The town which many people think of as the Gateway to Wales is Llangollen. It stands in the valley of the River Dee and tourists from Manchester and the north meet here those who have come from London and the Midlands along the A5 road. The little grey stone town is alive with excited people. They stand on the old bridge and watch the river as it swirls over the stones. Ahead lies the road to all the beauty of Snowdonia. Along the riverside are the ruins of Valle Crucis Abbey. Above the town is *Plas Newydd*, which was the home of the "Two Ladies of Llangollen" who were famous in the early nineteenth century for entertaining guests. People stay

The view from Llangollen Bridge

**Valle Crucis Abbey
(Llangollen)**

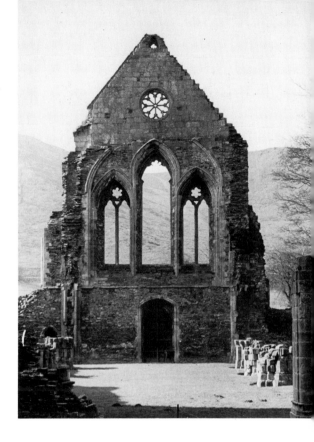

awhile and then hurry on to the mountains. It is a gay place. Last among the towns of Wales to be mentioned is Caernarfon. There was a Roman fort there. In 1283 Edward I built the magnificent castle standing on the shore of the Menai Straits. This was intended to be the palace of Edward's governor in Wales. The town retains some of its earlier dignity. More recently it was the scene of the investiture of H.R.H. Prince Charles as Prince of Wales at the castle on 1st July, 1969—a right royal note on which to leave this brief look at the towns of Wales.

Welsh Government, Education and Religion

When you go to Wales you feel you are visiting a separate country. In many villages the people talk in Welsh. When they speak English they give it a lilting accent. It does not sound like the English language which you hear in England. The signs are in Welsh and English.

In fact, Wales ceased to have a separate existence after Edward I defeated Llywelyn in 1282. Wales was then placed under the same laws as England, but there were no Welshmen in the English Parliament. Wales was a subject state. For the next two centuries there were rebellions and unrest.

When the Tudors came to the English throne this state of affairs was put right. The Act of Union in 1535 joined Wales and England on a fairer basis. Welsh members were elected to sit in the English Parliament.

Wales now returns thirty-eight members to the House of Commons in the United Kingdom Parliament. These form a Welsh Grand Committee which discusses subjects of Welsh interest. Another committee—the Select Committee on Welsh Affairs—has powers to investigate the work of government departments and public bodies in Wales.

The Secretary of State for Wales is responsible for Welsh Affairs. He is a member of the Cabinet. His department is called the Welsh Office. The department's main office is in Cardiff. It has branch offices throughout Wales and a small office in London. The department is responsible for agriculture, industry, planning, health and personal social services, local government, education and many other important matters.

The Conference of Heads of Government Offices in Wales, composed of all the Civil Service heads of Government Offices in Wales meets every two months so that the departments keep in touch with each other.

In this way Wales now has the benefit of being part of Britain and special attention is given to Welsh opinion.

Some Welsh people feel that because the Welsh Office is part of the government in London it cannot express the true opinion of Wales. They want to have a parliament in Wales. In some matters they have cause for complaint. In most things the Welsh people are no worse off than those in rural parts of England. People always feel that the government is doing the wrong thing and that they are not getting a fair deal. Perhaps the Welsh people would be happier if they could complain about their own government in Cardiff, rather than one in London!

At the moment the government is trying to meet the demands of the Welsh Nationalists. The government departments in Wales always include a number of Welsh-speaking staff so that business may be carried on in Welsh if preferred. Some official documents and forms are printed in Welsh and English.

EDUCATION
Education in Wales is on the same lines as in other parts

of Britain. Parents are required by law to see that their children receive efficient full-time education from the age of five to the age of sixteen.

At present there are about 484,000 pupils in primary and secondary schools in Wales. The schools vary greatly in size. In the country districts schools are small—some with less than twenty-five pupils. In the large cities of the south-east some of the schools are very large. There are twenty-six schools with more than 1,500 pupils.

Those reaching a sufficiently high standard go on to university. Some Welsh students go to the University of Wales. Some go to universities in England.

There were many early suggestions for a University of Wales, but nothing came of these, although Jesus College, Oxford, was founded by a Welshman in 1571 and it has always had an important place in Welsh education.

The University of Wales was founded in 1893. It now includes the colleges of Aberystwyth, Bangor, Swansea and Cardiff, the Welsh National school of Medicine in Cardiff, St. David's College, Lampeter, and the Institute of Science and Technology in Cardiff.

Some of these have done notable work through their associated bodies. The University College of Aberystwyth and its associated Plant Breeding Station has carried out some important work in the breeding of grasses. The Industrial Unit of the University College of Swansea has aided industry by research into many manufacturing problems.

Aberystwyth. The building in the foreground is the original main building of University College founded in 1872

In 1938 nearly all the students at the University of Wales came from Wales. By 1972 only about one-third of the students were Welsh.

RELIGION

You will by now know enough about the Welsh character to expect that the Welsh are religiously inclined. Since the Second World War, church-going has declined throughout Britain, but there is still support for the established churches in Wales, and there is growth in the newer denominations.

In the period after the Romans left Britain Christianity lingered on in Wales. Celtic Christian missionaries travelled from Ireland by way of South Wales to Britanny. The old style Christianity existed in Wales while England reverted to Pagan gods.

79

Later Christianity returned to South-east England and gradually spread across the country. The old and the new religions met in Wales. They did not agree on many details. It was not until the eighth century that the two streams of religion agreed upon the date when Easter should be celebrated.

The Bible was translated into Welsh in 1588 and this did much to preserve the Welsh language. Many people learnt to read Welsh in church.

The Welsh took up many of the non-conformist causes.

At one time there were many Welsh Quakers and during the period in the seventeenth century when this sect was persecuted a number of Welsh Quakers went to America. There are a number of places in that country which were founded by Welsh immigrants and some have Welsh names.

In the eighteenth century the great Methodist revival won many supporters in Wales. The Calvinistic Methodists gained more support than Wesley because they spoke Welsh, while he and his followers preached in English. In the 1890s it was estimated that over eighty per cent of the population of Wales were members of the chapels. Now the Calvinistic Methodists are known as the Presbyterian Church of Wales.

The Church of England was for a long time at a disadvantage in Wales because it was not Welsh. In 1920, the Welsh churches were disestablished (separated from the Church of England) and became the Church in Wales with an Archbishop at Bangor.

National Parks

What is a National Park? In some countries National Parks are owned by the Government and the public can wander anywhere they choose.

In Britain, National Parks are areas which are considered to be of special value because of their beauty and unspoilt nature. The land of the National Park often belongs to the people living there. Farmers continue to farm their land. Visitors can only go on roads, paths and stretches of open country as in other parts of Britain.

The aim of British National Parks is to protect the areas of best scenery and to help visitors enjoy them. Rules are made to guard the countryside from being spoilt by ugly buildings. Information centres are set up, staffed by experts who can advise visitors.

Since 1949 ten areas in Britain have been selected as National Parks. It says a great deal for the beauty of the Welsh countryside that three of these National Parks are in Wales. They cover nearly one-fifth of the whole country.

The three National Parks in Wales are Snowdonia, the Brecon Beacons and the Pembrokeshire Coast.

The Snowdonia National Park covers 2,188 square kilometres (845 square miles) of mountainous country in the north-west. It includes fourteen peaks over 915 metres (3,000 feet) high. One of these is Snowdon, 1,085 metres (3,560 feet), the highest mountain in England and Wales. Its rocky slopes provide a good training-ground for climbers. The team which first climbed Mount Everest in 1952, led by Sir John Hunt, trained there. There are also paths by which the ordinary walker can climb this great mountain. For the less energetic, a rack railway climbs from Llanberis to a station twenty metres (sixty-seven feet) below the summit.

In the Snowdonia National Park there are many Nature Trails and Forest Walks for visitors. Even without getting out of his car the motorist can see much of the fine mountain scenery. Some of the most exciting roads are the passes which climb over the shoulders of the mountains. Twelve of these are over 305 metres (1,000 feet) high. The highest is Bwlch-y-groes which was used as a test hill for early cars.

The Brecon Beacons National Park is in the south of mid Wales. It runs westwards from the Hereford and Worcester border and is 1,344 square kilometres (519 square miles) in area. It includes the Brecon Beacons and the Black Mountains.

The Brecon Beacons National Park has not the exciting mountains of Snowdonia, but it has a vast area of wild open moorland. It is an area where the walker gains much more enjoyment than the motorist, for there are few roads.

The Brecon Beacons Mountain Centre at Libanus near Brecon

The Offa's Dyke Long Distance Footpath goes along the ridge of the Black Mountains in the east. The grassy moorland of the Park is ideal for pony trekking and many young people enjoy this pastime. In the south of the Park there are extensive caves to explore.

The Pembrokeshire Coast National Park covers 583 square kilometres (225 square miles) of the south-west coast of Wales. It differs from the other National Parks in Wales by being mainly on the coast. For most of its length there are steep cliffs and rocky headlands. On the cliffs many seabirds nest. This is wild unspoilt coast. The Pembrokeshire Coast Path has been marked out for walkers.

The National Park goes right out to St. David's Head. North of this is an area of rolling upland. Stones were taken from this area to build Stonehenge, Britain's most famous stone circle on Salisbury Plain.

These three National Parks have some of the best scenery in Wales. They are all different. Each in its own way shows a new face of the attractions of Wales.

Holiday Wales

For many English people, Wales is a place for holidays. Some Welsh people would prefer their country to be less popular because they like to have a quiet life. But the visitors spend a great deal of money each year. Catering for holidays is one of the most important industries in Wales.

Some places offer only one type of holiday. Wales caters for every kind of holiday. If you cannot find what you want in Wales you must be very hard to please! There are beaches for bathing, rivers for fishing, mountains for climbing, the peace of lonely moors, and the gaiety of fun-fairs. The variety is so great that within half an hour you can be enjoying an altogether different type of holiday.

One of the first people to make Wales popular was George Borrow (1803-1881). He was a great walker and a good talker. He walked from Llangollen to Snowdonia and on down through mid Wales. He wrote of his experiences in *Wild Wales*. This book made Wales seem an exciting place. Many people went to see the country he described.

Snowdonia became a famous holiday area. Hotels were built at Betws-y-coed and other places. Artists found that there were many scenes to paint. There were so many visitors that in 1896 the Snowdon railway was built so that even the less energetic could reach the summit of the mountain.

The building of the Holyhead railway line along the North Wales coast opened up this area to those seeking holidays on the coast. Holiday resorts were developed. Llandudno had been merely a small parish in 1839. By 1869 it had grown to be what was described as "an elegant watering place with an esplanade two miles long". Other places developed and soon Wales could offer many types of holiday. Now it draws visitors from all over the world. It is especially popular with people in the cities of Liverpool and Manchester because they

84

Benllech Bay, Anglesey

can drive to Wales at the weekend in quite a short time.

Let's take a quick look round the coast.

Rhyl on the North Wales coast has a long sandy beach and provides fun-fairs, beauty parades, paddling-pools and all the gaiety you would expect at a big seaside resort. Colwyn Bay also has a very long seafront. Next comes Llandudno where a grand beach curves in an arc to Great Orme's Head and the sea is crystal blue. This strip of coast has an enviable record of sunshine. Yet only a short distance inland you are among the mountains.

The little island of Anglesey has as many faces as a diamond. From Beaumaris with its grand castle the coast goes round to the sandy Red Wharf Bay and then through a whole series of bays—some sandy, some rocky. There are said to be fifty safe beaches; enough for any holiday!

Along the curving coast of Cardigan Bay the resorts are smaller. Even the two largest—Barmouth and Aberystwyth— are quite small towns. They are popular with those who like more peaceful holidays.

South Wales offers another change. The coast has dramatic cliffs and rocky headlands. A very mild climate makes this area a favourite for early and late holidays. The biggest resort is Tenby which has a delightful harbour with little boats tossing on the tide. Even Swansea, though it is a large industrial centre, has a fine beach and the fascinating Gower Peninsula near by.

Inland holidays are quieter. The great mountains of Snowdonia draw many visitors every year. Further south are Cadair Idris and Plynlimmon. And there are great lakes and reservoirs.

Wales offers all types of interest and holidays. There are many caravan and camp sites. There are also fifty Youth Hostels for young walkers.

For the keen walker there is Offa's Dyke Long Distance Footpath. This is a 270-kilometre (168-mile) trail from Chepstow on the Severn estuary to Prestatyn on the North Wales coast. The path goes through some of the best of the border country and gives a wonderful walk. The Pembrokeshire Coast Path, in South Wales, is about the same length.

Among the lower hills pony-trekking is popular. The little Welsh ponies are sure-footed and young riders soon learn to handle them.

For older folk there are many well-known golf-courses.

The lakes and rivers are famous for salmon- and trout-fishing. Along the coast there is equally good sport. South Wales fishermen have caught cod and conger eels up to eighteen kilos (forty pounds). Sharks and tope weigh even more.

The Little Trains are a great attraction. These are narrow-gauge railways which were built to carry slate and other stone from quarries to the sea. When the quarries closed down the railway lines were also closed. Now railway enthusiasts have bought or rented them for use as passenger lines. The first to be saved was the Talyllyn Railway. This had been built in 1865 and ran over ten kilometres (6.5 miles) inland from Tywyn on Cardigan Bay. When the line was threatened with closure in 1951 it was taken over by a preservation society. Volunteers worked in every spare moment and now it is very busy.

The Rheidol Valley light railway at Devil's Bridge, Dyfed

The success of this line encouraged people to try to save more of the little railways. There are now nine of these concerns which provide a rare opportunity for people to ride in a train drawn by a steam engine. Most of the lines have exciting routes through the mountains giving passengers a chance to see beautiful countryside.

Even industry provides a holiday attraction in Wales: the Central Electricity Generating Board arranges trips round its giant power stations.

The old crafts provide another attraction. Welsh weavers, potters and makers of traditional wooden articles can be found in many villages and they are pleased to demonstrate their skills.

With so many things to see and do Wales offers everyone a holiday full of interest. No wonder it is becoming more popular every year.

The Llangollen Canal —a popular attraction for visitors to Wales

The Seven Wonders of Wales

Pistyll Rhaiadr and Wrexham Steeple,
Snowdon mountain without its people,
Overton Yew Trees, St. Winifred's Wells,
Llangollen Bridge and Gresford Bells.

That is the traditional list of the Seven Wonders of Wales.

PISTYLL RHAIADR is the highest waterfall in Wales. Its height is 73 metres (240 feet). The falls are in the heart of the Berwyn Mountains in North-east Wales and are difficult to find. The walker is rewarded with a dramatic sight.

WREXHAM STEEPLE. The poet was not a very observant architect. Wrexham Church has a pinnacled tower, not a steeple! It is 41 metres (135 feet) high and it is richly decorated with pinnacles. It is so imposing that some people say that it is too big for the church.

SNOWDON MOUNTAIN, the highest in Wales is worthy of its place in any list. Nowadays it has so many visitors that it is difficult to see it "without its people".

OVERTON YEW TREES. Overton is a village south of Wrexham in the north-east of Wales. The churchyard is crowded with twenty-one great yews. This is certainly the best collection in Wales.

ST. WINIFRED'S WELLS, HOLYWELL. Saint Winifred was a seventh-century saint. A local prince asked her to marry him. When she refused, the prince cut off her head with his sword.

Immediately the ground opened up and swallowed the prince. A spring gushed out at the place where Saint Winifred's head fell. The saint's uncle, Beuno, picked up her head and replaced it on her body. His prayers re-united it to her body and she came to life again. Ever since this has been a place of pilgrimage and many people have visited the well for cures.

LLANGOLLEN BRIDGE is a striking stone bridge with four arches. It was built in the fourteenth century by Dr. John Trevor, Bishop of St. Asaph. In 1873 the fourth arch was built to carry the road over the railway. The bridge was also widened.

GRESFORD BELLS are the church bells at Gresford near Wrexham in North-east Wales. There are eight of them. Such a large number is unusual for Wales.

This list of the Seven Wonders was made many years ago. It seems to have been made by someone from North Wales for every feature is in that part of the country.

After looking at Wales you may like to try to make your own list of the country's Seven Wonders.

To be fair, some features from Mid and South Wales should be included. Some of the new structures deserve to be considered.

Of the original Seven Wonders we must keep Snowdon. It is a grand sight and every change of weather gives it a new look.

Those who have visited Wales by road would also keep Llangollen Bridge in the list. It is a memorable spot on the journey and is sometimes called the Gateway to Wales.

The Swallow Falls, Betws-y-coed

Do you think that one of the nuclear power stations should be included? Or perhaps the pumped storage scheme at Ffestiniog, which enables the Central Electricity Generating Board to store the water until it is needed to make electricity? By the time you read this book it may be possible to visit the other larger pumped storage station at Dinorwig.

Although Pistyll Rhaiadr is the highest waterfall in Wales it is not the most impressive. This honour should go to the Swallow Falls at Betws-y-coed. The drop is not so great but the falls are much wider. After heavy rain the water surges down in a great foaming cascade.

No castles are included in the list of wonders although they are among the great sights of Wales. You may prefer Caernarfon Castle standing pleased with its reflection by the river. Or there is the lordly Raglan Castle. Perhaps you could include Conwy Castle? You could then add Conwy Bridge built in 1826 by Thomas Telford because the two go together so well.

Should one of Wales' delightful narrow-gauge railways be included? Then there is Tintern Abbey in the Wye Valley. This is a beauty spot which many people visit.

Conwy Castle and the bridge built in 1826 by Thomas Telford. Surely this is one of the wonders of Wales!

**Little boats
in the harbour
at Tenby**

You may want to include Tenby's fine harbour filled with little boats. Also in South Wales is the great harbour at Milford Haven where the biggest oil tankers can unload.

With so many things to choose from everyone will make his own list. Compare yours with those of others who have read this book.

At least you will agree that Wales is a country for Welshmen to be proud of!

Index

farming 22, 23–24, 49–53
Ffestiniog Pumped Storage Scheme
   60–61, 91
fishing 87
Flint 23, 27
Forest of Dean 25
forestry 53–54

George, David Lloyd 40
Gilbert de Clare, Earl 32
gold 48
government 9, 76, 77
Gower Peninsula 68–69, 86
Great Orme's Head 85
Gresford 90
Greville, Charles 69
Grosmont Castle 32
Gwent 12, 17

Harlech Castle 29
Henry V 11, 72
Henry VII 11
Herbert family 32
Holyhead 20
Hunt, Sir John 82

industry 40–48
iron and steel 12, 23, 25, 41–43, 46–47,
   71, 72

Jesus College, Oxford 78
John, Augustus 39
Jones, Tom 39

knitting 73

language 11–12, 14–16, 76–77, 80
laver bread 53
Lawrence, T. E. 38
Little Trains 87–88
Llandrindod Wells 73
Llandudno 84, 85
Llangollen 36, 74–75, 90
Llangollen International Eisteddfod 36
Llangollen, Ladies of 74
Llewellyn, R. 39
Lleyn Peninsula 22

Marches, Lords of 33
Men of Harlech 29
Menai Bridge 20
Merthyr Tydfil 41–42, 71–72
Methodists 80
Milford Haven 22, 41, 45, 63, 69–70, 93
Monmouth 32, 72–73
Monnow Bridge 72
mountains 12, 18–19

National Parks 13, 81–83
Newport 12, 23, 43, 70–71
Normans 11, 26, 32, 65, 70, 72, 73
Novello, Ivor 39
nuclear power stations 62–63

Offa 10
Offa's Dyke 10–11, 24
Offa's Dyke Long Distance Footpath
   83, 86
oil 13, 41, 45, 70
Overton 89

Pembroke Castle 30–31
Pembroke Castle National Park 83
Pembroke Coast Path 86
Pembroke Dock 22, 69
Pistyll Rhaiadr 89
Plynlimmon 25, 86
politicians 39–40
pony-trekking 86
population 9, 12
Portmeirion 39
Port Talbot 44, 46, 69, 72
potatoes 53
Powis Castle 33
Poyer John 31
Presbyterian Church of Wales 80
Prescelly 48
Prince of Wales, H.R.H. 29, 75

Quakers 80

Raglan Castle 32, 33, 92
railways 84
rainfall 12, 55